Tarumba

TARUMBA

The Selected Poems of Jaime Sabines

Edited and Translated by
Philip Levine and Ernesto Trejo

Sarabande Books

LOUISVILLE, KENTUCKY

Translations © 2007 by Philip Levine

FIRST EDITION

Managing Editor
Sarabande Books, Inc.
2234 Dundee Road, Suite 200
Louisville, KY 40205

Library of Congress Cataloging-in-Publication Data

Sabines, Jaime.
    Tarumba : the selected poems of Jaime Sabines / edited and translated by Philip Levine and Ernesto Trejo.
        p.   cm.
Parallel texts in English and Spanish.
ISBN-13: 978-1-932511-48-2 (pbk. : alk. paper)
ISBN-10: 1-932511-48-2 (pbk. : alk. paper)
I. Levine, Philip, 1928- II. Trejo, Ernesto. III. Title.
PQ7297.S2A24 2007
861'.64—dc22   2006015565

ISBN-13: 978-1-932511-48-2
ISBN-10: 1-932511-48-2

Cover image: *Mari in Embajadores,* by Antonio López García. Image courtesy of the artist and Marlborough Gallery, New York.

Cover and text design by Charles Casey Martin

Manufactured in Canada
This book is printed on acid-free paper.

Sarabande Books is a nonprofit literary organization.

**NATIONAL
ENDOWMENT
FOR THE ARTS**

This project is supported in part by an award from
the National Endowment for the Arts.

THE KENTUCKY ARTS COUNCIL

The Kentucky Arts Council,
a state agency in the Commerce Cabinet,
provides operational support funding for Sarabande Books
with state tax dollars and federal funding
from the National Endowment for the Arts,
which believes that a great nation deserves great art.

Contents

Foreword . . . . *xi*

PART ONE
From *Tarumba*

Prólogo 2

Introduction 3

"Tarumba, / Yo voy con las hormigas..." 4

"Tarumba, / I'm with the ants..." 5

"A la casa del día entran gentes y cosas..." 6

"People and things enter the house of the day..." 7

"Ay, Tarumba, tú ya conoces el deseo..." 8

"Yeah, Tarumba, you're already on fire..." 9

"La mujer gorda, Tarumba..." 10

"The fat woman wears..." 11

"En este pueblo, Tarumba..." 12

"In this town, Tarumba..." 13

"A caballo, Tarumba..." 14

"On horseback, Tarumba..." 15

"Oigo palomas en el tejado del vecino..." 16

"I hear pigeons on my neighbor's roof..." 17

"Si alguien te dice que no es cierto..." 18

"If someone tells you it's not for sure..." 19

"Sobre los ojos, sobre el lomo, cae..." 20

"It falls over your eyes..." 21

"Estos días, iguales a otros días de otros años..." 22

"These days, identical to other days of other years..." 23

"Quién sabe en qué rincón del trago..." 24

"In what corner of your drink..." 25

"Te puse una cabeza sobre el hombro..." 26

"I put a head on your shoulders..." 27

"¡Aleluya!" 30

"Hallelujah!" 31

"Esto es difícil..." 32

"This is difficult..." 33

"La primera lluvia del año moja las calles..." 34

"The first rain of the year darkens the streets..." 35

"¡En qué pausado vértigo te encuentras..." 36

"What a deliberate madness you feel!" 37

"Ahí viene un galope subterráneo..." 38

"Here comes the underground trot..." 39

"Cabalabula nuevamente..." 40

"Abracadabra again..." 41

"Vamos a cantar:..." 42

"Let's sing:..." 43

PART TWO

Está la ceniza 46

Ashes 47

Con los nervios saliéndome del cuerpo 48

With Nerves Trailing 49

Diario oficial (marzo de 70) 54

The Official Daily (March, 1970) 55

El estómago 56

My Stomach 57

Entresuelo 58

Between Floors 59

¿Hasta dónde entra el campo...? 62

At Night How Far...? 63

Rodeado de mariposas... 64

Surrounded by Butterflies... 65

Me gustan los aletazos... 66

It Pleases Me... 67

Pensándolo bien 68

Thinking It Over 69

El que se quedó sin dientes 70

The One with No Teeth 71

La luna 72

The Moon 73

Pasa el Lunes 76

Monday Passes 77

He aquí que estamos reunidos 78

So Here We Are 79

PART THREE

Tía Chofi 86

Aunt Chofi 87

De *Doña Luz* (Primera Parte) 92

From *Doña Luz* (Part One) 93

De *Algo sobre la muerte del mayor Sabines* (Segunda Parte) 104
From *Something on the Death of the Eldest Sabines* (Part Two) 105

Afterword *111*
The Author *117*
The Translator *119*

Foreword

Unlike most poetry written in Spanish, the poetry of Jaime Sabines has a great deal in common with much recent American poetry: his descriptions and images are accessible, and his vocabulary is colloquial. His most obsessive themes—death, love, time, loss—are familiar. His best poems are revelations of truths, odd truths, truths we immediately accept, which we have long suspected as truths but have never before heard articulated. And in his poems there is a curious lack of logical progressions. We are simply told: this follows that, this is how it is, this is how it feels, and if someone tells you it isn't so, tell him to come here...

To Octavio Paz, Sabines is one of the handful of poets that comprise the beginning of Modern Latin American poetry. To these poets the aim of the poem was not, as before, to invent, but rather to explore. The territory that attracted them most was neither the outer world nor the inner. It was that area where the internal and the external meet: the word. His charged, vernacular language often internalizes the world, and his emotions are not only observers but participants. Poet of the senses ("One has to touch and see arms and legs, / mouth, cheeks, wombs, / dissolving in the acid of death."), Sabines gives a human shape to his images, so that the cumulative effect is to give us a reflection of ourselves in the world, a world transformed into our spirit. His is a poetry that embraces and rejects the world, accepts and is horrified by death, praises and condemns our daily acts. In his poetry the world is a chaos upon which he does not try to impose an order or vision. Instead he moves out of the confines of the self to meet the sight and stink of ordinary life.

The chief preoccupations of Sabines' poetry are solitude, the anguish of living, and the limits imposed by time and death. His fierce skepticism is heightened by his horror of the end. The momentary pleasures which sustain him are shattered by his awareness of eventual destruction. The poet goes to a world in decay and finds that he himself is a symbol of brevity. What could transcend this man? Love and perhaps a defiance of the limits of life. The world of his poetry has been described as the realism of brothels, hospitals, and cantinas. And in fact they are often present, for his is a poetry that finds its human subjects at the limits of their lives.

It is hard to think of another living poet who knows so well the price we pay to endure in this world, which is the only world we have. All we have lost, each self we have cast away, each tender, vulnerable, abandoned cell of the soul, they are all gathered together in the presence of Tarumba, the poet's only faithful listener and constant companion. Together, Sabines, Tarumba, and the reader take the long voyage from first death, to minor death, to constant death, to final death, for that is the whole journey of the poetry of Sabines. Finally we stand with the poet, his words now ours: "We're all going to sell ourselves, Tarumba."

In a recent interview Sabines said, "No subject matter can be forced upon the poet. He must be a witness of his times. He must discover reality and recreate it. He should speak of that which he lives and experiences. I feel that a poet must first of all be authentic; I mean by this that there must be a correspondence between his personal world and the world that surrounds him. If you have a mystical inclination why not write about it? If you live alone and are afflicted by your solitude, why not speak about it, if it is yours? Poetry must bear witness to our everyday lives."

Sabines' best work always contains the elements of a fierce struggle.

His is a passage through untraveled streets, and the purpose never seems to require an explanation. (Do we explain poetry or does poetry explain us?) Sabines' poetry takes us to perfectly unexpected places that are somehow familiar, and there we see a world, his and ours, for the first time.

Ernesto Trejo, Mexico City, July 1977

Philip Levine, Fresno, California, July 1977

from
Tarumba

Prólogo

Estamos haciendo un libro,

testimonio de lo que no decimos.

Reunimos nuestro tiempo, nuestros dolores,

nuestros ojos, las manos que tuvimos,

los corazones que ensayamos;

nos traemos al libro,

y quedamos, no obstante,

más grandes y más miserables que el libro.

El lamento no es el dolor.

El canto no es el pájaro.

El libro no soy yo, ni es mi hijo,

ni es la sombra de mi hijo.

El libro es sólo el tiempo,

un tiempo mío entre todos mis tiempos,

un grano en la mazorca,

un pedazo de hidra.

Introduction

We are putting a book together,
a testimony of our untelling.
We gather our time and our grief,
our eyes, the hands we once had,
the hearts we rehearsed.
We come to this book
but at the end we are just bigger
and more unhappy than the book.
The cry is not the pain.
The song is not the bird.
This book is not me, nor my son,
nor the shadow of my son.
This book is only time,
a time among all my times,
just a kernel off the cob,
a chunk of eel.

Tarumba,

Yo voy con las hormigas

entre las patas de las moscas.

Yo voy con el suelo, por el viento,

en los zapatos de los hombres,

en las pezuñas, las hojas, los papeles;

voy a donde vas, Tarumba,

de donde vienes, vengo.

Conozco a la araña.

Sé eso que tú sabes de ti mismo

y lo que supo tu padre.

Sé lo que me has dicho de mí.

Tengo miedo de no saber,

de estar aquí como mi abuela

mirando la pared, bien muerta.

Quiero ir a orinar a la luz de la luna.

Tarumba, parece que va a llover.

Tarumba,

I'm with the ants
between the feet of flies.
I'm with the ground, the wind,
in men's shoes,
hoofs, leaves, papers;
I go where you go, Tarumba,
where you're from, I'm from.
I know the spider.
I know what you know about yourself
and what your father knew.
I know what you said about me.
I'm afraid not to know,
of being like my grandmother
looking at the wall, really dead.
I want to piss in moonlight.
Tarumba, it looks like it's going to rain.

A la casa del día entran gentes y cosas,
yerbas de mal olor,
caballos desvelados,
aires con música,
maniquíes iguales a muchachas;
entramos tú, Tarumba, y yo.
Entra la danza. Entra el sol.
Un agente de seguros de vida
y un poeta.
Un policía.
Todos vamos a vendernos, Tarumba.

People and things enter the house of the day,
stinkweeds,

the horses of insomnia,

catchy tunes,

window dummies that are girls;

you and I enter, Tarumba.

The dance enters. The sun enters.

An insurance agent enters

and a poet.

A cop.

We're all going to sell ourselves, Tarumba.

Ay, Tarumba, tú ya conoces el deseo.

Te jala, te arrastra, te deshace.

Zumbas como un panal.

Te quiebras mil y mil veces.

Dejas de ver mujer cuatro días

porque te gusta desear,

te gusta quemarte y revivirte,

te gusta pasarles la lengua de tus ojos a todas.

Tú, Tarumba, naciste en la saliva,

quién sabe en qué goma caliente naciste.

Te castigaron con darte sólo dos manos.

Salado Tarumba, tienes la piel como una boca

y no te cansas.

No vas a sacar nada.

Aunque llores, aunque te quedes quieto

como un buen muchacho.

Yeah, Tarumba, you're already on fire.
It drags you one way, then the other.
You grind like a honeycomb.
You explode a thousand times.
You go four days without a woman
because you like it that way,
the burning up and the coming back,
you like to pass the tongue of your eyes over them all.
Tarumba, you were born in spit,
born in God knows what hot goo.
Your curse was to grow only two hands.
Salty Tarumba, you've got the hide of a mouth
and you never wear out.
You're not gonna make it,
even though you cry, even though you sit perfectly still
like a good boy.

La mujer gorda, Tarumba,

camina con la cabeza levantada.

El cojo le dice al idiota: Te alcancé.

El boticario llora por enfermedades.

Yo los miro a todos desde la puerta de mi casa,

desde el agua de un pozo,

desde el cielo,

y sólo tú me gustas, Tarumba,

que quieres café y que llueva.

No sé qué cosa eres,

cuál es tu nombre verdadero,

pero podrías ser mi hermano o yo mismo.

Podrías ser también un fantasma,

o el hijo de un fantasma,

o el nieto de alguien que no existió nunca.

Porque a veces quiero decirte: Tarumba,

¿en dónde estás?

The fat woman wears

a proud face, Tarumba.

The cripple tells the idiot, "I caught up with you."

The pharmacist sobs at the sight of pain.

I watch them all from my doorway,

from the bottom of a well,

from heaven.

And you, Tarumba, are the only one I love;

you, who crave coffee and wish for rain.

I don't know what you are,

or what your real name is,

but you could be my brother or myself.

Or you could be a ghost,

or the child of a ghost,

the grandchild of someone who never was.

Sometimes I feel like asking

Where are you, Tarumba?

En este pueblo, Tarumba,

miro a todas las gentes todos los días.

Somos una familia de grillos.

Me canso.

Todo lo sé, lo adivino, lo siento.

Conozco los matrimonios, los adulterios,

las muertes.

Sé cuándo el poeta grillo quiere cantar,

cuándo bajan los zopilotes al mercado,

cuándo me voy a morir yo.

Sé quiénes, a qué horas, cómo lo hacen,

curarse en las cantinas,

besarse en los cines,

menstruar,

llorar, dormir, lavarse las manos.

Lo único que no sé es cuándo nos iremos,

Tarumba, por un subterráneo,

al mar.

In this town, Tarumba,

I watch everyone every day.

We are a family of crickets.

I get tired.

I know everything, I guess it, I feel it:

the marriages, the adulteries,

the deaths.

I know when the cricket poet wants to sing,

when the buzzards come to market,

when I am going to die.

I know which ones, at what time, how they do it:

healing themselves in the bars,

kissing in moviehouses,

menstruating.

They cry, sleep, wash their hands.

The only thing I don't know, Tarumba,

is when we are leaving through the underground tunnel,

for the sea.

A caballo, Tarumba,

hay que montar a caballo

para recorrer este país,

para conocer a tu mujer,

para desear a la que deseas,

para abrir el hoyo de tu muerte,

para levanter tu resurrección.

A caballo tus ojos,

el salmo de tus ojos,

el sueño de tus piernas cansadas.

A caballo en el territorio de la malaria,

tiempo enfermo,

hembra caliente,

risa a gotas.

A donde llegan noticias de vírgenes,

periódicos con santos,

y telegramas de corazones deportivos como una bandera.

A caballo, Tarumba, sobre el río,

sobre la laja de agua, la vigilia,

la hoja frágil del sueño

(cuando tus manos se despiertan con nalgas),

y el vidrio de la muerte en el que miras

tu corazón pequeño.

A caballo, Tarumba,

hasta el vertedero del sol.

On horseback, Tarumba,

you've got to ride a horse

to cover this ground,

to know your woman,

to want the one you want,

to open the hole of your death,

to get your resurrection off the ground.

On horseback your eyes,

the psalm of your eyes,

the sleep in your tired legs.

On horseback in the malarial lands,

sick time,

hot woman,

drops of laughter.

Where news of virgins arrives,

newspapers with saints,

and telegrams of sporting hearts like banners.

On horseback, Tarumba, over the river,

over the flat stones of water, the vigil,

the fragile leaf of sleep,

(when your hands waken around an ass)

and the mirror of death in which you see

your little heart.

On horseback, Tarumba,

as far as the sinkhole of the sun.

Oigo palomas en el tejado del vecino.
Tú ves el sol.
El agua amanece,
y todo es raro como estas palabras.
¿Para qué te ha de entender nadie, Tarumba?
¿Para qué alumbrarte con lo que dices
como con una hoguera?
Quema tus huesos y caliéntate.
Ponte a secar, ahora, al sol y al viento.

I hear pigeons on my neighbor's roof.
You see the sun.
Water breaks like dawn
and everything is strange, like these words.
Why should they understand you, Tarumba?
Why should your words be a bonfire,
shedding their light on you?
Ignite your bones and warm up.
Dry yourself now, in the sun and the wind.

Si alguien te dice que no es cierto,

dile que venga,

que ponga sus manos sobre su estómago y jure,

que atestigüe la verdad de todo.

Que mire la luz en el petróleo de la calle,

los automóviles inmóviles,

las gentes pasando y pasando,

las cuatro puertas que dan al este,

las bicicletas sin nadie,

los ladrillos, la cal amorosa,

las estanterías a tu espalda cayéndose,

las canas en la cabeza de tu padre,

el hijo que no tiene tu mujer,

y el dinero que entra con la boca llena de mierda.

Dile que jure, en el nombre de Dios invicto

en el torneo de las democracias,

haber visto y oído.

Porque ha de oír también el crimen de los gatos

y un enorme reloj al que dan cuerda pegado a tu oreja.

If someone tells you it's not for sure,

tell him to come here,

to put his hands over his stomach and swear,

to bear witness to the whole truth.

To see the light in the oily street,

the stopped cars,

the people passing and passing,

the four doors which face the East,

the empty bicycles,

the bricks, the affectionate quicklime,

the bookshelves tumbling behind you,

the gray hairs on your father's head,

the son your wife never had,

and the money that walks in with its mouth full of shit.

In the name of the undefeated God

in the contest of the democracies,

tell him to swear he's seen and heard.

Because he's also got to hear the crime of the cats

and keep his ears glued to the big clock they keep winding.

Sobre los ojos, sobre el lomo, cae

como una bestia lenta,

pesa,

respira el agua,

se extiende en la cara de las cosas,

agobia.

Nace en el corazón del aire

y envejece en el tiempo,

tesoro de las piedras,

riñón del árbol,

casa de los ancianos,

trompeta de la muerte.

Animal disperso,

se congrega bajo el sol,

abre la tierra, chupa,

despelleja los ríos,

espanta a las hormigas,

duerme al gato,

y a ti te hace un nudo de víbora

o un huevo aplastado.

Este calor benigno, reparador del mundo,

te entierra a golpes, Tarumba-clavo.

It falls over your eyes
and your back like a beast, heavy
and slow.
It inhales water
and spreads on the surface of things.
It burdens you.
Born in the heart of the air,
it ages in time;
treasure of the stones,
kidney of the tree,
house of the senile,
trumpet of death.
A scattered animal,
it gathers under the sun.
Cracking the earth it sucks
and skins the rivers,
terrifies the ants
and puts the cat to sleep.
It can ring you like a snake
or make a smashed egg
out of you.
This benign heat, restorer of the world,
buries you with heavy blows, Tarumba-spike.

Estos días, iguales a otros días de otros años,

con gentes iguales a otras gentes,

con las mismas horas y los mismos muertos,

con los mismos deseos,

con inquietud igual a la de antes;

estos días, Tarumba, te abren los ojos,

el viento largo y fino te levanta.

No pasa nada, ni estás solo.

Pasas tú con el frío desvelado

y pasas otra vez. No sabes dónde,

a dónde, para qué.

Oyes recetas de cocina,

voceadores, maullidos.

¡Fiestas de la barriga, navidad, año nuevo,

qué alegres estamos,

qué buenos somos!

Tú, Tarumba, te pones tus alas de angel

y yo toco el violín.

Y el viejo mundo aplaude con las uñas

y derrama una lágrima, y sonríe.

These days, identical to other days of other years,
with people identical to other people,
the same hours and the same dead.
Your wishes are the same
and the old unrest is there.
These days are opening your eyes, Tarumba.
The long fine wind lifts you,
nothing happens and you are not alone.
With the sleepless cold you pass
and pass again. You don't know where
to go and have no reason to move.

You listen to recipes,
paperboys, howling.
Celebrations of our full bellies, Christmas,
New Year's.
We are so joyful
and so good!
Tarumba, you put on your angel wings
and I will play the violin.
The old world applauds with its fingertips,
sheds a tear, and smiles.

Quién sabe en qué rincón del trago,
a qué horas, pensaste
que la vida era maravillosa.
Te pusiste tu cara de idiota
y te alegraste.
Sentiste que ibas a ser papá.
Amaste lo elemental. Hablaste
a las piedras, y sacaste del bolsillo
el resplandor de santo con que te ves tan bien.
Todos dijeron: ¡A un lado!
y pasaste en silencio, sobre la adoración.

Desde esa vez andas de mal humor.
Te molestan las gentes
y aún dentro del sueño
no miras nada.
Adelgazas como el viento
y oyes voces con el corazón.
Eres, casi, tu estatua.
¡Alabado sea Dios!

In what corner of your drink,
at what time, did you think that
life was wonderful?
You put on your idiot's face
and became cheerful.
You felt you were going to be a daddy.
You loved the elemental. You spoke
to stones and took out of your pocket
the splendor of a saint so becoming on you.
They all said "step aside!"
and you passed by in silence, worshipped.

But ever since you've been sour.
People annoy you
and even in dreams
you see nothing.
Like the wind you're getting thinner
and hear voices in your heart.
You are almost a statue of yourself.
Praise the Lord!

Te puse una cabeza sobre el hombro
y empezó a reír;
una bombilla eléctrica,
y se encendió.
Te puse una cebolla
y se arrimó un conejo.
Te puse mi mano
y estallaste.

Di cuatro golpes sobre tu puerta
a las doce de la noche
con el anillo lunar,
y me abrió la sábana que tiene cuerpo de mujer,
y entré a lo oscuro.

En el agua estabas como una serpiente
y tus ojos brillaban con el verde que les corresponde a esas horas.
Entró el viento conmigo
y le subió la falda a la delicia, que se quedó inmóvil.
El reloj empezó a dar la una
de cuarto en cuarto, con una vela en la mano.
La araña abuelita tejía
y la novia del gato esperaba a su novio.
Afuera, Dios roncaba.
Y su vara de justicia, en manos del miedo ladrón,
dirigía un vals en la orquesta.
Me soplaste en el ombligo

I put a head on your shoulders
and it started to laugh,
a bulb,
and it lit up.
I put an onion,
and a rabbit drew near,
I put my hand on you
and you went off.

At midnight
I knocked four times on your door
with the ring around the moon,
and the sheet with a woman's body opened
and I entered the darkness.

In the water you were like a serpent
and your eyes glittered with the right green for those hours.
The wind entered with me
and went up your skirt right to the joy, that didn't even move.
Holding a candle, the clock began to strike one
from room to room.
Grandmother spider weaved
and the cat's girl waited for her sweetheart.
Outside God snored.
And in the hands of fear, the thief, His rod of justice
led the orchestra in a waltz.
You breathed into my navel

y me hinché y ascendí entre los ángeles.

Pero tuve tiempo de ponerme la camisita

y los zapatitos con que me bautizaron.

Tú quedaste como un cigarro ardiendo en el suelo.

and I puffed up and ascended among the angels.

But I had time to put on my little shirt

and the shoes in which they baptized me.

You stayed on the ground smoldering like a cigarette.

¡Aleluya!

¿Qué pasa?

Hay una escala de oro invisible

en la que manos invisibles ascienden.

Llevo una flor de estaño en el ojal de la camisa.

Estoy alegre.

Me corto un brazo y lo dejo señalando el camino.

Una mujer embarazada se sienta sobre una silla y aplaude

al jugador de tenis que juega solo.

Tomo el café del sábado.

Me destapo los ojos de un balazo

¡y arriba!

Hallelujah!

What's going on?
There is a scale of unseen gold
where invisible hands rise.
I wear a tin flower in my button hole.
I am happy.
I cut off one of my arms and leave it pointing the way.
A pregnant woman sits in a chair and cheers
the tennis player serving to himself.

I drink Saturday's coffee.
I open my eyes with a bullet.
Wake up!

Esto es difícil

pero si pones atención aprenderás a hacerlo.

Te sacas la lengua poco a poco

y la enrollas en el carrete de hilo negro.

Guardas tus ojos en un barril de vino

y en la bodega, junto a los estantes,

llamas a Dios tres veces:

Cabalabula-bulacábala-bulabo.

(Para el domingo: dominicus-eructur-mintus.

Para el jueves: Jovis-jorovis-multilovis.)

Entonces, sobre la tierra,

los hombres empiezan a volar como los ángeles.

En los mercados venden la felicidad.

Los niños son los jueces.

En todas las esquinas hay una caja de música

y una pila de agua.

Los gatos pasean del brazo a las ancianas ratas

y tú, delgado como una sonrisa, sueñas.

     (Paréntesis: el antiguo mirar

     de una mujer de negro.

     Una mujer antigua,

     un negro sin tiempo.

     Sonata en tiempo negro

     escrita para mujer desvestida de negro.)

Esto se echó a perder, Tarumba.

This is difficult,

but if you pay attention you can do it.
Stick out your tongue slowly
and wind it around the spool of black thread.
Put your eyes away in a wine barrel
in the cellar, face the shelves
and address God thrice:
Cabalabula-bulacabala-bulabo.
(On Sundays: Dominicus-eructur-mintus.
On Thursdays: Jovis, jorovis, multilovis.)
At that moment, in the world,
men start to fly like angels.
The markets sell happiness.
Children are judges.
On every corner there is a music box
and a fountain.
Cats stroll on the arms of old rats
and you, thin as a smile, dream.

(Parenthesis: the ancient glance
of a woman in black.
An ancient woman,
a timeless black.
Sonata in black time
written for woman undressed in black.)

This is a flop, Tarumba.

La primera lluvia del año moja las calles,

abre el aire,

humedece mi sangre.

¡Me siento tan a gusto y tan triste, Tarumba,

viendo caer el agua desde quién sabe,

sobre tantos y tanto!

Ayúdame a mirar sin llorar,

ayúdame a llover yo mismo sobre mi corazón

para que crezca como la planta del chayote

o como la yerbabuena.

¡Amo tanto la luz adolescente

de esta mañana

y su tierna humedad!

¡Ayúdame, Tarumba, a no morirme,

a que el viento no desate mis hojas

ni me arranque de esta tierra alegre!

The first rain of the year darkens the streets,

swells the air,

and waters my blood.

I feel so alive and so blue, Tarumba,

watching the rain come down from who knows where

onto all this and all that.

Help me to see without tears,

help me to rain down on my own heart

so that it can bear like the gourd vine

or the yerbabuena.

I love the boyish light

of this morning

and the soft sea air.

Help me, Tarumba, to not die,

don't let the wind scatter my leaves

or tear up my roots from this happy earth.

¡En qué pausado vértigo te encuentras,
qué sombras bebes en qué sonoros vasos!
¡Con qué manos de hule estás diciendo adiós
y qué desdentada sonrisa echas por delante!
Te miro poco a poco tratando de quererte
pero estás mojado de alcohol
y escupes en la manga de tu camisa
y los pequeños vidrios de tus ojos se caen.
¿A dónde vas, hermano?
¿De qué vergüenza huyes?,
¿de qué muerte te escondes?
Yo miro al niño que fuiste,
cómo lo llevas de la mano
de cantina a cantina, de un hambre a otra.
Me hablas de cosas que sólo tu madrugada conoce,
de formas que sólo tu sueño ha visto,
y sé que estamos lejos, cada uno en el lugar de su miseria,
bajo la misma lluvia de esta tarde.
Tú no puedes flotar, pero yo hundirme.
Vamos a andar del brazo, como dos topos amarillos,
a ver si el dios de los subterráneos nos conduce.

What a deliberate madness you feel!
What shadows you drink in clinking glasses!
With what rubbery hands you wave good-bye
and what a toothless smile blooms before you!
I look at you and try feebly to desire you
but you're drenched in alcohol
and you spit on your own sleeve
and the little windows fall from your eyes.
Where are you going, brother?
What shame are you escaping?
What death are you hiding from?
I see the child you were,
how you took him by the hand
from bar to bar, from one hunger to another.
You talk to me of things you know only at dawn,
of figures only your dreams have seen,
and I know we're miles apart, each rooted in his own misery,
under the same rain of this afternoon.
You can't float, but I could sink.
Let's walk arm in arm, like two jaundiced moles,
and see if the Lord of Tunnels will guide us.

Ahí viene un galope subterráneo,

viene un mar rompiendo,

viene un ventarrón de Marte.

(Alguien ha de explicarme

por qué no suceden tantas cosas.)

Viene un golpe de sangre

desde mis pies de barro,

vienen canas en busca de mi edad,

tablas flotando para mi ataúd.

(El Rey de Reyes come un elote, espera,

se prueba unas sandalias de hoja de plátano.)

Viene mi abuelita Chus,

que cumplió trece desaños,

trece años en la muerte,

trece años para atrás, para lo hondo.

Me visitan Tony, Chente, mi tía Chofi,

y otros amigos enterrados.

Pienso en Tito, jalando de la manga a su muerte

y ésta no haciendo caso.

Viene Challito dolorosa

con su hoja de menta

y con un caballito para mi hijo.

Y viene el aguacero más grande de todos los tiempos

y el miedo de los rayos,

y tengo que subirme a un arca transformado en buey

para la vida dichosa que nos espera.

Here comes the underground trot,

here comes the rupturing sea,

the storm winds off Mars.

(Can't someone tell me why

so many things don't make it?)

Here comes a smack of blood

up from my mud feet.

Here come my gray hairs looking for middle age,

the planks floating toward my coffin.

(While waiting the King of Kings munches sweet corn

and tries on banana-peel sandals.)

Here comes my little granny Chus,

who's turned thirteen nothings old,

thirteen years in the grave,

thirteen years in the wrong direction, down.

Tony, Chente, my aunt Chofi, all here,

my buried friends come to see me.

I think of Tito, dragging his death by the sleeve,

his death that couldn't care less.

Here comes Challito in pain,

chewing a mint leaf

and with a toy horse for my kid.

Here comes the worst downpour of all time

and the fear of lightning,

I've got to turn myself into the ox and climb on

the ark bound for the good life that awaits us all.

Cabalabula nuevamente.

Algo tiene que decirse a estas horas.

Voy en busca de pan.

Voy a ganar dinero.

Voy buscando un lugar dónde caerme muerto.

Traigo la canasta del mercado

con verduras y carne

y una bolsa de arroz y un manojito de flores silvestres,

pero vengo pensando en mi marido que no llegó a dormir anoche.

Yo voy a la escuela

con mi cuaderno sin tareas.

Yo estoy de paso y nomás miro.

Y este mezquino dolor en la cabeza

metiéndose como un ratón en su agujero.

¿En dónde estará?, ¿qué estará haciendo?

Me muero de mujer a estas horas.

Cabalabula, Tarumba.

En mi vida de perro camino pegado a la pared.

El viento se tuesta la espalda al sol.

Con la mano más larga de las que tengo

me busco, husmeo mi cráneo en el cajón de la basura.

Abracadabra again.

At this hour I have to say something.
I'm off to the bakery,
out to make money or
to find a spot to drop dead.
In my shopping bag,
vegetables, meat,
rice, and a small bunch of wildflowers.
My mind, however, is set on my man
who didn't come to bed last night.

I go to school
without my homework.
I'm just passing through and like to look.
A headache squeezes into my brain,
a mouse into his hole.
Where can she be? What could she be doing?
This late I'm hard up for a woman.
Abracadabra, Tarumba.
All my life I have walked scratching
myself on the walls
like a dog.
The sun burns the wind's back.
With my longest hand I look for myself,
I nose my skull into the trash can.

41

Vamos a cantar:

tararí, tatá.
El viejito cojo
se duerme con sólo un ojo.
El viejito manco
duerme trepado en un zanco.
Tararí, totó.
No me diga nada usted:
se empieza a dormir mi pie.
Voy a subirlo a mi cuna
antes que venga la tía Luna.
Tararí, tuí,
tuí.

Let's sing:

tarrara, boom da.

Little old gimper

falls asleep with one eye.

Little old one-arm

snoozes perched on a stilt.

Rarrara, boom boo.

Don't tell me nothing:

my foot begins to drowse.

I'm going to lug it up to my cradle

before Auntie Moon gets here.

Tarrara, boom di,

boom, di.

Está la ceniza

Está la ceniza en el plato
sobre la cama, la almohada,
la libreta, la ropa, mi cuerpo,
escribiendo estas palabras.
En el techo, la lámpara
eléctrica, la ceniza,
la huella de algún alma,
una sombra, una araña.
Hay cuatro o cinco paredes
o seis, o espejos, o aguas
puestas de pie, y pintadas
unas manos despintadas,
unos rostros hacia dentro,
unas calaveras con máscaras.
El geranio se pasea en el patio
al lado de la rosa blanca
y el drenaje en silencio
se traga el chorro de aire de la casa.
Le doy la vuelta al mundo
cuando me caigo de la cama.
Soy el héroe de la corneta,
el de la boca desdentada.

Ashes

There are ashes on my plate,
on the bed, the pillow, my clothes,
my body. Ashes are writing
these words. On the ceiling, the lightbulb,
ashes, the ashes are something left
of a soul. A shadow, a spider.
There are four or five walls,
maybe six, or mirrors.
There's water on its feet,
a portrait of confused hands.
There are faces turned inward
and masked skulls.
In the patio
the geranium takes the air
on the arm of the white rose
and the drain quietly swallows
the stream of breath
that the house exhales.
When I fall off my bed
I have circled the world.
I am the trumpet-wielding hero,
the toothless one.

Con los nervios saliéndome del cuerpo

Con los nervios saliéndome del cuerpo como hilachas,
como las fibras de una escoba vieja,
y arrastrando en el suelo, jalando todavía
el fardo de mi alma,
cansado, todo, más que mis propias piernas,
hastiado de usar mi corazón del diario,
estoy sobre esta cama y a estas horas
esperando el derrumbe,
la inminente caída que ha de sepultarme.
(Hay que cerrar los ojos como para dormir
y no mover ni una hoja de tu cuerpo.
Esto puede ocurrir de un momento a otro:
estarse quieto.
Pañuelos de aire giran lentamente,
sombras espesas rascan las paredes,
el cielo te chupa a través del techo.)

Mañana te has de levantar de nuevo
a caminar entre las gentes.
Y amarás el sol y el frío,
los automóviles, los trenes,
las casas de moda, y los establos,
las paredes a que se pegan los enamorados
al entrar la noche, como calcomanías,

With Nerves Trailing

I'm out on this bed
with nerves trailing from my body like frayed threads,
like the whiskers of an old broom,
dragging on the floor, tugging
at the bundle of my soul.
I'm dead tired. More tired of using my heart
every day than my legs.
I wait at all hours for the landslide,
the scheduled collapse, that will bury me.
(You have to shut your eyes as in sleep
and hold every leaf of your body still.
This can occur from one moment to the next,
this stilling oneself.
Handkerchiefs of air are slowly being spun,
heavy shadows scrape the walls,
heaven is sucking you up through the roof.)

Tomorrow you'll rise again
and walk among your people.
You'll love the sun, the cold,
the cars, trains,
the fancy shops and the stables,
the walls to which lovers plaster themselves
like posters at dusk,

los parques solitarios en que se pasean las desgracias

con la cabeza baja, y los sueños se sientan a descansar,

y algún novio la busca bajo la falda,

mientras la sirena de la ambulancia de la hora

de entrar a la fábrica de la muerte.

Amarás la milagrosa ciudad y en ella el campo soñado,

el río de las avenidas iluminadas por tanta gente que quiere lo mismo,

las puertas de los bares abiertas, las sorpresas de las librerías,

el estanco de flores, los niños descalzos

que no quieren ser héroes de la miseria,

y las marquesinas, los anuncios,

la prisa de los que no tienen a dónde ir.

Amarás el asfalto y la buhardilla

y las bombas para el drenaje y las grúas

y los palacios y los hoteles de lujo

y el césped de las casas donde hay un perro guardián

y dos o tres gentes que también se van a morir.

Amarás los olores de las fritangas

que en la noche atraen como una luz a los hambrientos,

y tu cabeza se irá detrás del perfume

que alguna mujer deja en el aire como una boa suspendida.

Y amarás las ferias mecánicas

donde los pobres llegan al vértigo y a la risa,

y el zoológico, donde todos se sienten importantes,

y el hospital, donde el dolor hace más hermanos

que los que puede hacer la pobreza,

y las casas de cuna, y las guarderías en que juegan los niños,

the empty parks where sorrow walks

head down and your dreams slump on a bench,

where the lover slides his hand under a skirt

as the ambulance whistles a new shift

into the factories of death.

You'll love the magic city and in her the land you dreamed,

the blazing streets burned by all those who love them,

the open doors of bars, the surprises of the bookshops,

the flower stands, the barefoot kids

who don't want to be the noble poor,

the movie marquees, the ads,

the rush of those who have nowhere to go.

You'll love the pavement below and the attics above,

the drainage pumps and the tow trucks,

the palaces and the first-class hotels

and the watch dogs in the yards of those houses

where two or three are going to die.

You'll love the smell of doughnuts

that signal the poor all night like a beacon,

and your head will be turned by some woman's perfume

left in the air like a floating boa.

You'll love the amusement parks

where the poor get dizzy and laugh,

the zoo where we all feel superior,

the hospitals where pain

makes more brothers than poverty,

the orphanages and nurseries where the kids play,

y todos los lugares en que la ternura se asoma como un tallo

y las cosas todas te ponen a dar gracias.

Pasa tu mano sobre la piel de los muebles,

quita el polvo que has dejado caer sobre los espejos.

En todas partes hay semillas que quieren nacer.

(Como una escarlatina te va a brotar, de pronto, la vida.)

all those places where tenderness nudges forth like a sprout

and all things lead you to give thanks.

Run your hand over the surfaces of furniture,

wipe away the dust that has fallen on your mirror.

Everywhere there are seeds that want to bear.

(Life bursts from you, like scarlet fever, without warning.)

Diario oficial
(marzo de 70)

Por decreto presidencial: el pueblo no existe.
El pueblo es útil para hablar en banquetes:
"Brindo por el pueblo de México,"
"Brindo por el pueblo de Estados Unidos."

También sirve el pueblo para otros menesteres literarios:
escribir el cuento de la democracia,
publicar la revista de la revolución,
hacer la crónica de los grandes ideales.

El pueblo es una entidad pluscuamperfecta
generosamente abstracta e infinita.
Sirve también para que jóvenes idiotas
aumenten el área de los panteones
o embaracen las cárceles
o aprendan a ser ricos.

Lo mejor de todo lo ha dicho un señor Ministro:
"Con el pueblo me limpio el culo."
He aquí lo máximo que puede llegar a ser el pueblo:
un rollo de papel higiénico
para escribir la historia contemporánea con las uñas.

The Official Daily
(March, 1970)

By presidential decree: the people do not exist.
The people are useful for banquet talk.
"A toast to the people of Mexico."
"A toast to the people of the United States."

The people are also useful for other literary needs:
writing the story of democracy,
editing the magazine of the revolution,
making the chronicle of high ideals.

The people are a pluperfect entity,
generously abstract and infinite.
They are useful also for stupid young people
to increase the acreage of cemeteries,
to fatten up the prisons,
or to learn to make money.

The ultimate was said by a Secretary of State,
"I wipe my ass with the people."
Such is the utmost the people may aspire to:
a roll of toilet paper
to write contemporary history with their nails.

El estómago

El estómago, los intestinos, el corazón, los nervios, creo que hasta los riñones se me están echando encima. Necesito otro cuerpo. Necesito un cuerpo de metal para que aguante. O bien un árbol, o una piedra. Tiene que ser resistente al venenoso amor, a la insondable fatiga, al alcohol tutelar, a la congregación de los presagios, al ritmo impúdico, vicioso de la vida.

La paranoia se desnuda al pie de la cama y baila silenciosamente. Me pongo a ver un programa de vaqueros en la televisión.

La muerte no importa. Lo que importa es la lluvia, afuera, la insensible tarde, la vida despidiéndose inútilmente.

My Stomach

My stomach, my intestines, my heart, my nerves, and I think even my kidneys are turning on me. I need another body. One of metal to endure. Or else a tree or a rock. It has to be able to bear up under the poison of love, the impenetrable weariness, the tutelage of alcohol, the congregation of omens, the shameless and dull rhythm of life.

Paranoia unrobes at the foot of my bed and dances quietly. I tune a western on TV.

Death is not important. What matters is this rain, this afternoon that couldn't care less, this life saying good-bye to no avail.

Entresuelo

Un ropero, un espejo, una silla,
ninguna estrella, mi cuarto, una ventana,
la noche como siempre, y yo sin hambre,
con un chicle y un sueño, una esperanza.
Hay muchos hombres fuera, en todas partes,
y más allá la niebla, la mañana.
Hay árboles helados, tierra seca,
peces fijos idénticos al agua,
nidos durmiendo bajo tibias palomas.
Aquí, no hay una mujer. Me falta.
Mi corazón desde hace días quiere hincarse
bajo alguna caricia, una palabra.
Es áspera la noche. Contra muros, la sombra,
lenta como los muertos, se arrastra.
Esa mujer y yo estuvimos pegados con agua.
Su piel sobre mis huesos
y mis ojos dentro de su mirada.
Nos hemos muerto muchas veces
al pie del alba.
Recuerdo que recuerdo su nombre,
sus labios, su transparente falda.
Tiene los pechos dulces, y de un lugar
a otro de su cuerpo hay una gran distancia:
de pezón a pezón cien labios y una hora,

Between Floors

A closet, a mirror, a chair,
not a single star, my room with its window
giving onto the usual night, and I
with no appetite, with my bubble gum
and my dream, my hope. There are men
out there everywhere, and beyond them fog
and morning. There are icy trees, dry earth,
fish frozen exactly like ice.
Nests sleeping under warm doves.
There is no woman here. Just me alone.
For days now I've wanted to throw
myself under any caress or any word.
It's rough tonight. Against the walls
the darkness crawls as slowly as the dead.
That woman and I were held together by water.
Her skin over my bones,
and my eyes filled with her vision.
We died into each other so many times
at the break of day.
I recall that I recall her name, her lips,
the skirt I could see through.
Such sweet breasts! From one place
of her body to another there are great distances:
from one nipple to another there are

de pupila a pupila un corazón, dos lágrimas.
Yo la quiero hasta el fondo de todos los abismos,
hasta el último vuelo de la última ala,
cuando la carne toda no sea carne, ni el alma
    sea alma.
Es preciso querer. Yo ya lo sé. La quiero.
¡Es tan dura, tan tibia, tan clara!

Esta noche me falta.
Sube un violín desde la calle hasta mi cama.
Ayer miré dos niños que ante un escaparate
de manequíes desnudos se peinaban.
El silbato del tren me preocupó tres años,
hoy sé que es una máquina.
Ningún adiós mejor que el de todos los días
a cada cosa, en cada instante, alta
la sangre iluminada.

Desamparada sangre, noche blanda,
tabaco del insomnio, triste cama.

Yo me voy a otra parte.
Y me llevo mi mano, que tanto escribe y habla.

one hundred lips and one hour. From one eye
to the other there is a heart and two tears.
I want her to the depth of each abyss,
to the last flight
of the last wing, when the whole flesh
will no longer be flesh nor the soul
soul. Love is necessary. I found that out.
I love her, this tough, warm, true woman.

Tonight I'm without her.
From the street music rises and enters my bed.
Yesterday I watched two kids combing their hair
mirrored on a store window of naked dummies.
The train's call obsessed me for three years
and now I know it's only a machine.
There is no better good-bye than the one
you say to everything every day, right
up to the fullness of the blood.

Here alone, soft night,
the smoke of insomnia, the sad bed.

I'm going somewhere else.
I'm taking this hand that writes and talks on and on.

¿Hasta dónde entra el campo...?

¿Hasta dónde entra el campo a la ciudad, de noche?,
el aire de los cerros,
las estrellas, las nubes sigilosas?
Cuando las fábricas descansan
y los motores duermen como algunos hombres,
paso a paso, los árboles penetran a las calles macizas,
y el frío se extiende como una sábana de aire,
sube a las azoteas, se enconde en los zaguanes,
aquieta el agua de las fuentes.
La hojarasca, la ardilla, los rumores, la alfalfa,
los eucaliptos y los álamos, las legumbres adolescentes,
los insectos, el viento, hasta las sombras vienen
a limpiar la ciudad, a poseerla.
(Cuando llega la luz, el campo se retira
como un enamorado culpable y satisfecho.)

At Night How Far...?

At night how far does the countryside enter the city?
The air blown in from the hills,
the stars, the silent clouds?
While the factories drowse
and the motors dream human dreams,
the trees slip step by step through the narrow streets
and the cold settles down like a sheet of air
on the rooftops, buries itself in doorways
and silences the flow of the fountains.
The dried leaf, the squirrel, the murmur, the alfalfa,
the eucalyptus and the aspens, the unripened sprouts,
the insects, the wind, even the shadows have come
to clean the town, to claim it.
(When day breaks the country sneaks off
like a lover, guilty and satisfied.)

Rodeado de mariposas...

Rodeado de mariposas negras como almas
y de agudos puñales que practican los muertos,
condescendiendo a ser buen hombre y buen soldado,
pater et filius admirabilis,
me canonizo en el espléndido amanecer del mundo.

Soy el conocedor de los misterios,
el doloroso sonriente,
el que guarda las llaves de las estrellas.
Oficio en el zoológico
ante leones urbanos y monos posgraduados en psicología.
Soy el Rey de la Selva Civilizada,
receptáculo de la luna,
vaso de la alegría.

(Vienen vientos del norte con húmedos imanes
arrastrando y creciendo.
Pájaros perdidos como sueños.)

Abandonado estoy, sarna de Job,
paciencia mía.

Surrounded by Butterflies . . .

Surrounded by butterflies as dark as souls
and the honed switchblades the dead carry,
I agree to be a good guy and a good soldier
pater et filius admirabilis
I canonize myself in the world's glorious dawn.

I myself am the master of the mysteries,
the smiling sufferer
who guards the keys to the stars.
Among the urban lions and the monkeys
with doctorates in psychology
I run the zoo.
I am the king of the forest of civilization,
I am the moon's urn,
the cup of joy.

(From the north the winds blow their wet magnets,
dragged and swollen.
Birds lost in dreams.)

Abandoned, I am left with Job's hives,
with my own patience.

Me gustan los aletazos …

Me gustan los aletazos de la lluvia sobre los lomos de la ciudad flotante.

Desciende el polvo. El aire queda limpio, atravesado de hojas de olor, de pájaros de frescura, de sueños. El cielo recibe a la ciudad naciente.

Tranvías, autobuses, camiones, gentes en bicicleta y a pie, carritos de colores, vendedores ambulantes, panaderos, ollas de tamales, parrillas de plátanos horneados, pelotas de un niño a otro: crecen la calles, se multiplican los rumores en las últimas luces del día puesto a secar.

Salen, como las hormigas después de la lluvia, a recoger la miga del cielo, la pajita de la eternidad que han de llevarse a sus casa sombrías, con pulpos colgando del techo, con arañas tejedoras debajo de la cama, y con un fantasma familiar, cuando menos, detrás de alguna puerta.

Gracias te son dadas, Madre de las Nubes Negras, que has puesto tan blanca la cara de la tarde y que nos has ayudado a seguir amando la vida.

It Pleases Me . . .

It pleases me, the way the rain beats its wings on the shoulders of the floating city.

The dust descends. The air is cleansed and spiked by perfumed leaves, by the fresh winds of birds, by dreams. The sky receives the just-born city.

Streetcars, buses, trucks, men on bicycles and on foot, carts of many colors, walking vendors, bakers, pots of tamales, grills of baked bananas, balls going from one kid to another: the streets swell, the voices of the multitudes grow in the last light of the day hung out to dry.

Like ants after the rain stops, they come out to grasp the crumbs of heaven, the small straw of eternity to carry off to their dark houses, with giant squid hanging from the roof, with spiders weaving under the bed, and with at least one familiar ghost waiting behind a door.

My thanks to you, Mother of Black Clouds, who have drained the face of the afternoon and helped us to go on with our lives.

Pensándolo bien

Me dicen que debo hacer ejercicios para adelgazar,
que alrededor de los 50 son muy peligrosos la grasa y el cigarro,
que hay que conservar la figura
y dar la batalla al tiempo, a la vejez.

Expertos bien intencionados y médicos amigos
me recomiendan dietas y sistemas
para prolongar la vida unos años más.

Lo agradezco de todo corazón, pero me río
de tan vanas recetas y tan escaso afán.
(La muerte también ríe de todas estas cosas.)

La única recomendación que considero seriamente
es la de buscar mujer joven para la cama
porque a estas alturas
la juventud sólo puede llegarnos por contagio.

Thinking It Over

They tell me I have to exercise and lose weight,
that at my age—fifty—it's dangerous to be overweight and smoke,
that I have to slim down
and wage the battle against aging.

The well-intentioned experts and my dear doctor friends
recommend diets and regimens
to prolong my life for decades.

I sincerely thank them and secretly laugh
at their useless recipes and ploys.
(Death also laughs at all this.)

The one recommendation I take seriously
is to find a young woman to take to bed
because at this altitude
youth will only come back as an infection.

El que se quedó sin dientes...

El que se quedó sin dientes
no puede bailar.
El que se quedó sin ojos
no puede decir "bon jour madame".
"El día está bonito:
hágame el favor de morirse".
El que se quedó sin calzones
no puede caminar entre la muchedumbre.
El que se quedó sin nadie
no puede llorar.
El que se quedó sin nadie
no puede llorar. No puede llorar. No puede llorar.
(Esto debe repetirse tres veces).

El que se quedó sin almohada
debe dormir sobre las nalgas de una puta.
El que se quedó sin techo
que aprenda el abecedario de las estrellas;
el que sin pared,
a resistir el viento.
El que se quedó sin carne,
a la carnicería.
El que se quedó sin Dios:
a la iglesia del sagrado silencio.

The One with No Teeth

The one with no teeth
can't dance.
The one without eyes
can't say, "Bon jour, Madame."
"It's a beautiful day,
do me a favor and croak."
The one without pants
can't walk among the crowds.
The one who has no one
can't cry.
The one without anyone
can't cry. Can't cry. Can't cry.
(You have to say that three times.)

The one who lies down without a pillow
has to sleep on a whore's ass.
The one without a roof over his head
must recite the alphabet of the stars;
the one without a wall
must stop the wind.
The one without meat
must go to the butcher.
The one without God
must attend the church of sacred silence.

La luna

La luna se puede tomar a cucharadas
o como una cápsula cada dos horas.
Es buena como hipnótico y sedante
y también alivia
a los que se han intoxicado de filosofía.
Un pedazo de luna en el bolsillo
es mejor amuleto que la pata de conejo:
sirve para encontrar a quien se ama,
para ser rico sin que lo sepa nadie
y para alejar a los médicos y las clínicas.
Se puede dar de postre a los niños
cuando no se han dormido,
y unas gotas de luna en los ojos de los ancianos
ayudan a bien morir.

Pon una hoja tierna de la luna
debajo de tu almohada
y mirarás lo que quieras ver.
Lleva siempre un frasquito del aire de la luna
para cuando te ahogues,
y dále la llave de la luna
a los presos y a los desencantados.
Para los condenados a muerte

The Moon

You can take the moon every two hours
either with a tablespoon or in capsules.
It works as a tranquilizer and a sedative
and it also relieves
a hangover from OD-ing on philosophy.
In your pocket a ray of moonlight
is a surer charm than a rabbit's foot:
with it you'll find the beloved
or get secretly rich
and avoid doctors and clinics.
It calms and sweetens children
who can't fall asleep,
and a few drops of the moon in the eyes of the old
can help them find a good death.

Put a fresh leaf of the moon
under your pillow
and you'll see whatever you want to see.
Always carry a small flask of moon air
to breathe when you go under,
and donate the key to the moon
to prisoners and the others without hope.
For anyone condemned to death,

y para los condenados a vida
no hay mejor estimulante que la luna
en dosis precisas y controladas.

for anyone condemned to life
there's no better medicine than the moon
taken regularly in the prescribed dose.

Pasa el lunes...

Pasa el lunes y pasa el martes
y pasa el miércoles y el jueves y el viernes
y el sábado y el domingo,
y otra vez el lunes y el martes
y la gotera de los días sobre la cama donde se quiere dormir,
la estúpida gota del tiempo cayendo sobre el corazón aturdido,
la vida pasando como estas palabras:
lunes, martes, miércoles,
enero, febrero, diciembre, otro año, otro año, otra vida.
La vida yéndose sin sentido, entre la borrachera y la concienca,
entre la lujuria y el remordimiento y el cansancio.

Encontrarse, de pronto, con las manos vacías,
con el corazón vacío,
con la memoria como una ventana hacia la obscuridad,
y preguntarse: ¿qué hice?, ¿qué fui?, ¿en dónde estuve?
Sombra perdida entre las sombras,
¿cómo recuperarte, rehacerte, vida?

Nadie puede vivir de cara a la verdad
sin caer enfermo o dolerse hasta los huesos.
Porque la verdad es que somos débiles y miserables
y necesitamos amar, ampararnos, esperar, creer y afirmar.

Monday Passes

Monday passes and Tuesday passes
and Wednesday goes by and Thursday and Friday
and Saturday and Sunday also,
and again Monday and Tuesday,
the days leaking onto the bed where you search for sleep,
the dumb drip of time leaking into your stunned heart,
life passes just as these words pass:
Monday, Tuesday, Wednesday,
January, February, December, another year, still another, another life.
Life slips by without your noticing, between bouts of boozing and fits
    of conscience,
between lust, remorse, exhaustion.

Suddenly you find yourself empty-handed,
empty-hearted,
with a memory like a window that looks out on darkness
and you ask yourself: "What happened? Who was I? Where am I?"
A shadow lost among shadows,
how can you find yourself? How can you take up your life?

Because we're weak, miserable creatures
who need love, who need secrecy, hope, belief, affirmation,
to live looking truth in the face
is to sicken, to ache down to the bones.

No podemos vivir a la intermperie
en el solo minuto que nos es dado.

¡Qué hermosa palabra "Dios", larga
y útil al miedo, salvadora!
Aprendamos a cerrar los labios del corazón
cuando quiera decirla,
y enseñémosle a vivir en su sangre,
a revolcarse en su sangre limitada.

No hay más que esta ternura que siento hacia ti, engañado,
porque algún día vas a abrir los ojos
y mirarás tus ojos cerrados para siempre.
No hay más que esta ternura de mí mismo
que estoy abierto como un árbol,
plantado como un árbol, recorriéndolo todo.

He aquí la verdad: hacer las máscaras,
recitar las voces, elaborar los sueños.
Ponerse el rostro del enamorado,
la cara del que sufre,
la faz del que sonríe,
el día lunes, y el martes, y el mes de marzo
y el año de la solidaridad humana,
y comer a las horas lo mejor que se pueda,
y dormir y ayuntar,

We can't survive in the world
for even that brief moment given us.

What a beautiful word "God," so full,
so useful when you're scared, such a savior!
We must learn to still the heart
when it wants to say that word,
we must teach it to live on its own blood,
to survive on its own limit of blood.

Cheated, you feel sorry only for yourself
because someday you'll open your eyes
and see only your own eyes closed forever.
For myself alone I too feel pity,
for I am branched open like a tree,
rooted like a tree, and surveying everything.

So here's how it's done: you put on your mask,
assume your voice, embroider your dreams.
Put on the face of a lover,
the wounded face,
the contented smile,
Monday, and Tuesday, and the month of March,
and the year of human solidarity,
you eat on the hour as best you can,
and sleep and make love,

y seguirse entrenando ocultamente para el evento final del que no habrá testigos.

and go on secretly rehearsing for the final act

that no one will witness.

He aquí que estamos reunidos

He aquí que estamos reunidos
en esta casa como en el Arca de Noé:
Blanca, Irene, María y otras muchachas,
Jorge, Eliseo, Oscar, Rafael . . .
Vamos a conocernos rápidamente
y a fornicar y a olvidarnos.
El buey, el tigre, la paloma, el lagarto y el asno, todos
juntos bebemos, y nos pisamos y nos atropellamos
en esta hora que va a hundirse en el diluvio nocturno.
Relámpagos de alcohol cortan la oscuridad de las pupilas
y los truenos y la música se golpean entre las voces desnudas.
Gira la casa y navega hacia las horas altas.
¿Quién te tiene la mano, Magdalena, hundida en las almohadas?
¡Qué bello oficio el tuyo, de desvestirte
y alumbrar la sala!
¡Haz el amor, paloma, con todo lo que sabes:
tus entrenadas manos, tu boca, tus ojos,
tu corazón experto!
He aquí la cabeza del día, Salomé,
para que bailes delante de todos los ojos en llamas.
¡Cuidado, Lesbia, no nos quites ni un pétalo de las manos!
Sube en el remolino la casa y el tiempo sube
como la harina agria. ¡Hénos aquí a todos, fermentados,
brotándonos por todo el cuerpo el alma!

So Here We Are

So here we are together

in this house like in Noah's Ark:

Blanca, Irene, Maria, and other girls,

Jorge, Eliseo, Oscar, Rafael ...

Let's get down right away

and fuck and forget each other.

The ox, the tiger, the dove, the lizard, and the jackass, all of us

booze together, and knock each other over and rush to it

in this hour about to sink into the night flood.

Bolts of alcohol slice the darkness of the pupils

and the thunder and the music storm each other among the naked voices.

The house spins and sails toward the small hours.

Collapsed in the pillows, Magdalena, who holds your hand?

What a beautiful job you do, undressing yourself

and lighting up the room!

Keep loving, baby, with everything you know:

your trained hands, your mouth, your eyes,

your professional heart!

Here's the head of the day, Salome,

so you can dance before all our eyes on fire.

Careful, Lesbia, don't take one petal from our hands!

The house rises in the whirlwind and time rises

like sourdough. Here we are, all of us, fermenting,

our souls growing out all over our bodies.

Tía Chofi

Amanecí triste el día de tu muerte, tía Chofi,
pero esa tarde me fui al cine e hice el amor.
Yo no sabía que a cien leguas de aquí estabas muerta
con tus setenta años de virgen definitiva,
tendida sobre un catre, estúpidamente muerta.
Hiciste bien en morirte, tía Chofi,
porque no hacías nada, porque nadie te hacía caso,
porque desde que murió abuelita, a quien te consagraste,
ya no tenías qué hacer y a leguas se miraba
que querías morirte y te aguantabas.
¡Hiciste bien!
Yo no quiero elogiarte como acostumbran los arrepentidos
porque te quise a tu hora, en el lugar preciso,
y harto sé lo que fuiste, tan corriente, tan simple,
pero me he puesto a llorar como una niña porque te moriste.
¡Te siento tan desamparada,
tan sola, sin nadie que te ayude a pasar la esquina,
sin quién te dé un pan!
Me aflige pensar que estás bajo la tierra
tan fría de Berriozábal,
sola, sola, terriblemente sola,
como para morirse llorando.
Ya sé que es tonto eso, que estás muerta,

Aunt Chofi

I felt sad the morning you died, aunt Chofi,
but that afternoon I went to a movie and made love.
I didn't know that far away from here you were dead,
at seventy, a virgin for good.
You were stretched out on a cot, stupidly dead.
You did the right thing, aunt Chofi,
you had nothing to do and no one listened;
you devoted your life to your mother, and since she died
you had nothing to do, and it was obvious
you wanted to die but held back.
You did the right thing.
I don't want to eulogize you like the remorseful
because I loved you at the right time,
at the right place, and I know too well
what you were—ordinary, simple,
but still I cried like a girl because you are dead.
I feel you are so lonely and helpless,
no one will help you cross the streets,
no one will hand you a piece of bread.
It hurts me to think of you
under the cold ground of Berriozábal,
lonely, so lonely,
and all I can do is cry.
I know this is silly, that you are dead,

que más vale callar,
¿pero qué quieres que haga
si me conmueves más que el presentimiento de tu muerte?

Ah, jorobada, tía Chofi,
me gustaría que cantaras
o que contaras el cuento de tus enamorados.
Los campesinos que te enterraron sólo tenían
tragos y cigarros,
y yo no tengo más.
Ha de haberse hecho el cielo ahora con tu muerte,
y un Dios justo y benigno ha de haberte escogido.
Nunca ha sido tan real eso en lo que creíste.
Tan miserable fuiste que te pasaste dando tu vida
a todos. Pedías para dar, desvalida.
Y no tenías el gesto agrio de las solteronas
porque tu virginidad fue como una preñez de muchos hijos.
En el medio justo de dos o tres ideas que llenaron tu vida
te repetías incansablemente
y eras la misma cosa siempre.
Fácil, como las flores del campo
con que las vecinas regaron tu ataúd,
nunca has estado tan bien como en ese abandono de la muerte.
Sofía, virgen, antigua, consagrada,

that it is better to stop,

but what can I do

if your death moves me more than the fear

of your death.

Ah, Chofi, hunchback,

I would like to hear you sing

or tell the tale of your suitors.

The peasants who dug your grave

had only a bottle and a pack of cigarettes;

and that's all I have.

Since your death there has to be a heaven,

a just and benign God must have chosen you.

You had so little and you spent it all

giving yourself to others. Destitute,

you asked so you could give.

Yours wasn't the frown of an old maid

because your virginity was like a pregnancy

      for child after child.

Two or three ideas filled your life

and you repeated them over and over,

you were always the same.

Uncomplicated, like the wildflowers

your neighbors sprinkled on your grave.

Neglected even in death,

you never had it better than now.

Chofi, virgin, ancient, consecrated,

debieron enterrarte de blanco

en tus nupcias definitivas.

Tú que no conociste caricia de hombre

y que dejaste llegaran a tu rostro arrugas antes que besos,

tú, casta, limpia, sellada,

debiste llevar azahares tu último día.

Exijo que los ángeles te tomen

y te conduzcan a la morada de los limpios.

Sofía virgen, vaso transparente, cáliz,

que la muerte recoja tu cabeza blandamente

y que cierre tus ojos con cuidados de madre

mientras entona cantos interminables.

Vas a ser olvidada de todos

como los lirios del campo,

como las estrellas solitarias;

pero en las mañanas, en la respiración del buey,

en el temblor de las plantas,

en la mansedumbre de los arroyos,

en la nostalgia de las ciudades,

serás como la niebla intocable, hálito de Dios que despierta.

Sofía virgen, desposada en un cementerio de provincia,

con una cruz pequeña sobre tu tierra,

estás bien allí, bajo los pájaros del monte,

y bajo la yerba, que te hace una cortina para mirar al mundo.

they should have buried you in white

for your final wedding vows.

You, who never felt the hands of a man,

whose face preferred wrinkles to kisses,

you, chaste, pure, sealed, you

should have carried wedding blossoms on your final day.

I demand that the angels lead you

to the abode of the pure.

Chofi, virgin, transparent vessel, chalice,

may your death hold you softly by your temples

and shut your eyelids like a mother

while she sings an endless song.

Everyone will forget you, the way

they forget the wild lilies,

the way they forget the lonely stars;

but in the morning, when the ox breathes,

the shrubs tremble, the creeks flow tamely,

and the cities feel the old nostalgia,

you will be fog, untouchable, the breath of God, awakening.

Chofi, virgin, wedded in a village cemetery,

with a small cross over the mound of your grave,

it is a good place for you, under the wild birds,

under the grasses that open like a curtain

so you may behold the world.

De Doña Luz *(Primera Parte)*

A Juan Camacho

I

Acabo de desenterrar a mi madre, muerta hace tiempo. Y lo que desenterré fue una caja de rosas: frescas, fragantes, como si hubiesen estado en un invernadero.

¡Qué raro es todo esto!

IV

Creo que estuvo en la tierra algunos años. Creo que yo también estuve en la tierra. ¿Cuál es esa frontera?, ¿qué es lo que ahora nos separa?, ¿nos separa realmente?

A veces creo escucharla: tú eres el fantasma, tú la sombra. Sueña que vives, hijo, porque es hermoso el sueño de la vida.

V

En un principio, con el rencor de su agonía, no podía dormir. Tercas, dolorosas imágenes repetían su muerte noche a noche. Eran mis ojos sucios, lastimados de verla; el tiempo del sobresalto y de la angustia. ¡Qué infinitas caídas agarrado a la almohada, la oscuridad girando, la boca seca, el espanto!

Pero una vez, amaneciendo, la luz indecisa en las ventanas, pasó su mano sobre mi rostro, cerró mis ojos. ¡Qué confortablemente ciego estoy de ella! ¡Qué bien me alcanza su ternura! ¡Qué grande ha de ser su amor que me da su olvido!

From Doña Luz *(Part One)*

To Juan Camacho

I

I've just unearthed my mother, who's been dead for some time. And what I dug up was a box of roses: fresh, fragrant, as though they'd been in a hot house.

This is all so strange!

IV

I think she was on earth a while. I think I was too. Where's the border? What separates us now? Does anything?

Sometimes I think I hear her speaking: You are a ghost, a shadow. Dream that you are alive, son, because the dream of life is beautiful.

V

At first I couldn't sleep, out of hatred for her agony. In stubborn, painful images I saw her die night after night. My eyes were soiled and hurt from watching her in that time of shock and anguish. What bottomless falls! I clutched the pillow, the whirling darkness, dry mouthed I clutched the terror.

But once at dawn the light paused in the window, passed its hand over my face and closed my eyes. Now I'm comfortably blind of her! Her tenderness reaches me anyway! How great her love must be to give me her forgetfulness!

VI

Fue sepultada en la misma fosa de mi padre. Sus cuerpos reposarán juntos hasta confundirse, hasta que el tiempo diga ¡basta!

(¡Qué nostalgia incisiva, a veces, como ésta!)

¿En dónde seré enterrado yo? Me gustaría cuidar mis funerales: nadie llorando, los encargados del oficio, gente decente. De una vez solo hasta un lugar lejano, sin malas compañías. O incinerado, estupendo. Cualquier río, laguna, charco, alcantarilla: todo lugar sagrado.

No me acostumbro a vivir.

VIII

Si tú me lo permites, doña Luz, te llevo a mi espalda, te paseo en hombros para volver a ver el mundo.

Quiero seguir dándote el beso en la frente, en la mañana y en la noche y al mediodía. No quiero verte agonizar, sino reír o enojarte o estar leyendo seriamente. Quiero que te apasiones de nuevo por la justicia, que hables mal de los gringos, que defiendas a Cuba y a Vietnam. Que me digas lo que pasa en Chiapas y en el rincón más apartado del mundo. Que te intereses en la vida y seas generosa, enérgica, espléndida y frutal.

Quiero pasear contigo, pasearte en la rueda de la fortuna de la semana y comer las uvas que tu corazón agitaba a cada paso.

Tú eres un racimo, madre, un ramo, una fronda, un bosque, un campo sembrado, un río. Toda igual a tu nombre, doña Luz, Lucero, Lucha, manos llenas de arroz, viejecita sin años, envejecida sólo para parecerte a los vinos.

VI

She was buried in the same grave as my father. Their bodies will lie together until they're fused, until time says, Enough!

(What an incisive nostalgia at times like this!)

Where will I be buried? I'd like to arrange my own funeral: no one crying, and the officials decent-looking people. Once and for all alone in a far off place with no bad company. Or cremated, stupendous! Any river, lagoon, puddle, drain would do: any sacred place.

I can't get used to living.

VIII

If you'll let me, Doña Luz, I'll carry you on my back, I'll give you a ride on my shoulders so you can see the world again.

I want to go on giving you a kiss on the forehead, morning, noon, and night. I don't want to see you dying, but laughing or getting angry or reading seriously. I want you to get excited again about justice, to bitch about the gringos, to stand up for Cuba and Vietnam. To tell me what's going on in Chiapas and in the farthest corner of the world. I want you to be interested in life, to be generous and energetic, splendid and fruitful.

I want to take a walk with you, to take you for a ride on the week's wheel of fortune, and to eat the grapes your heart used to stir with each step.

You are a cluster of grapes, a branch, a leaf, a forest, a sown field, a river. Everything alike in your name, Doña Luz, Lucero, Lucha, hands full of rice, old woman without years, like wine deepening with age.

XI

Dame la mano, o cógete del brazo, de mi brazo. Entra al coche. Te llevaré a dar el último paseo por el bosque.

Querías vivir, lo supe. Insistías en que todo era hermoso, pero tu sangre caía como un muro vencido. Tus ojos se apagaban detrás de ti misma. Cuando dijiste "volvamos" ya estabas muerta.

¡Qué dignidad, qué herencia! Nos prohibes las lágrimas ahora. No nos queda otro remedio que ser hombres.

XIII

Decías que una mariposa negra es el alma de un muerto. Y hace muchos días que esta mariposa no sale de la casa. Hoy temprano la he visto sobre el cristal de la ventana, aleteando oscuramente, y dije: ¡Quién sabe! ¿Por qué no habías de ser una mariposa rociando mi casa con el callado polen de sus alas?

XIV

Tú conoces la casa, el pequeño jardín: paredes altas, estrechas, y allí arriba el cielo. La noche permanece todavía sobre la tierra y hay una claridad amenazante, diáfana, encima. La luz penetra a los árboles dormidos (hay que ver la isla de los árboles dormidos en la ciudad dormida y quieta). Se imaginan los sueños, se aprende todo. Todo está quieto, quieto el río, quieto el corazón, de los hombres. Los hombres sueñan.

Amanece sobre la tierra, entre los árboles, una luz silenciosa, profunda.

Me amaneces, dentro del corazón, calladamente.

XI

Give me your hand, or take my arm. Get into the car. I'll take you for your last ride through the forest.

You wanted to live, I knew that. You insisted that everything was beautiful, but your blood fell like a defeated wall. Your eyes died out behind you. When you said "let's go back" you were already dead.

But what dignity! What a legacy! You forbid us to cry now. There's nothing left for us but to be men.

XIII

You used to say that black butterflies are the souls of the dead. The days go on, and this butterfly hasn't left my house. Earlier today I saw it fluttering darkly on the window, and I said, Who knows! Why wouldn't you be a butterfly sprinkling my house with the quiet pollen of your wings?

XIV

You know the house, the small garden: tall, narrow walls and the sky above. Night persists over the earth, and there is a menacing clarity, transparent, above. Light penetrates the sleeping trees (you should see the island of sleeping trees in the city that sleeps and is still). Dreams are imagined, one learns everything. Everything is quiet, the river, the hearts of men, quiet. Men are dreaming.

Dawn rises over the earth, among the trees, a silent and profound light.

You dawn, quietly, in my heart.

XVI

"Cuando reviva mi abuelita, voy a acusar a Julio con ella," me dio a entender la Pipi hoy en su media lengua. "¿Veldá, papá?"

—Sí, hijita. Cuando reviva tu abuelita le va a dar unas nalgadas a Julio para que no te moleste.

Y me quedé pensando que todavía no es posible. Son los meses del frío. Habrá que esperar la primavera para que nazcas de la amorosa tierra, bajo los árboles luminosos, en el aire limpio.

XIX

Niña muerte, descansa
en nuestros brazos quietos.

En la sombra, descansa
junto a nuestro cuerpo.
Cómete mis ojos
para mirar adentro,
acaba mis labios,
mi boca, el silencio,
bébete mi alma,
bébete mi pecho,
niña muerte, mía,
que yo te mantengo.
La tierra está negra,
mi dolor es negro.
Vacía está mi caja,
vacío está mi cuerpo.

XVI

"When grandma comes back to life I'm going to tell on Julio," Pipi told me today in her broken language. "Right, Papa?"

—Yes, sweetheart. When your grandma comes back she'll give Julio a spanking so he won't pester you anymore.

And I kept thinking, it can't happen yet. These are the cold months. We'll have to wait until spring for you to be born from the loving earth, under the luminous trees, in the pure air.

XIX

Rest, Little Death,
here in our quiet arms.

In the darkness, rest
beside this body of ours.
Swallow my eyes
so I can see inside,
take my lips,
my mouth, my silence,
drink my soul,
my breast too,
my Little Death,
and I'll feed you.
The earth is black;
my pain, black.
My coffin is empty,
my body is empty.

Niña muerte, gota
de rocío en mi pelo.

XXII

¿Es que el Viejo está muerto y tú apenas recién morida? (¿Recién
parida? ¿palpitante en el seno de la muerte? ¿aprendiendo a no ser?
¿deslatiendo? ¿Cómo decir del que empieza a contra al revés una
cuenta infinita?)

¿Es que hay flores frescas y flores marchitas en el rosal oscuro
de la muerte?

¿Por qué me aflijo por ti, como si el Viejo ya fuese un experto
en estas cuestiones y tú apenas una aprendiz?

¿Es que han de pasar los años para que los muertos saquen de su
corazón a los intrusos? ¿Cuándo me arrojarás, tú también, de tu tumba?

XXIII

El cráneo de mi padre ha de ser pequeño y fino. Sin dientes: se los
quitaron hace tiempo. Las cuencas de los ojos no muy grandes. La
frente tersa, sin daño, ascendiendo graciosamente; la herradura del
maxilar sólida, maciza.

Si pudiera ponerle unos ojos al destino, le pondría los suyos, de
una vez que me dijo: somos polvo.

Somos huesos un tiempo. Harina de la piedra que ha de quedarse
inmóvil.

Siento que no podré morirme hasta no tener en mis manos un
momento el cráneo de mi padre. Es como una cita que tenemos: lo
más amado de nosotros dos.

My Little Death, a drop

of dew in my hair.

XXII

Is it that the Old Man is dead and you are just dead? (Just reborn?
Vibrating in the heart of death? Your heart beating backwards toward
birth? What do you call someone who starts beating backwards toward
infinity?)

Is it that there are fresh flowers and wilted ones on the dark
rosebush of death?

Why do I grieve for you, as though the Old Man were already an
expert in these matters and you barely an apprentice?

Is it that years will have to pass before the dead rid their hearts
of intruders? When will you throw me out of your grave?

XXIII

My father's skull must be small and delicate. Without teeth; they were
taken out years ago. The eye sockets also small. The forehead smooth,
undamaged, ascending gracefully; the horseshoe of the jaw solid, firm.

If I could put eyes on fate, I'd put the ones he wore when he
told me, We are dust.

For a time we are bones. Flour of the stone that will not grind.

I feel I won't be able to die until I've held my father's skull in my
hands a moment. It's like an appointment we have, the one most
beloved by both of us.

101

XXIV

Todo esto es un cuento, lo sabemos. He querido hacer un poema con tu muerte y he aquí que tengo la cabeza rota, las manos vacías. No hay poesía en la muerte. En la muerte no hay nada.

Tú me das el poema cuando te sientas a mi lado, cuando hablamos. ¡En sueños! ¿No serán los sueños sólo la parte subterránea de este río que amanece cargado de esencias? ¿No serán el momento de conocer para siempre el corazón oculto de la tierra?

¿Quién canta? El que lloró hace rato. ¿Quién va a vivir ahora? Los que estábamos muertos.

El paralítico se levanta todos los días a andar, mientras el ciego atesora la luz para siempre.

Por eso el hambriento tiene el pan, y al amoroso no lo sacia la vida.

XXIV

All this is just a story, we know that. I've tried to make a poem out of your death, and here I am—my brains worked to nothing—empty-handed. There is no poetry in death. There's nothing in death.

You give me the poem when you sit at my side, and we talk. In dreams! Aren't dreams only the undercurrent of this river that arrives at dawn, filled with essences? Aren't they the time when we know, outside of time, the hidden heart of the earth?

Who's singing? The one who just a moment ago wept? Who's going to live now? We who were dead.

The paralytic gets up every day to walk, while the blind man stores up light forever.

That's why the hungry have bread, and why life leaves the loving hungry.

De Algo sobre la muerte del mayor Sabines
(Segunda Parte)

Mientras los niños crecen, tú, con todos los muertos
poco a poco te acabas.
Yo te he ido mirando a través de las noches
por encima del mármol, en tu pequeña casa.
Un día ya sin ojos, sin nariz, sin orejas,
otro día sin garganta,
la piel sobre tu frente, agrietándose, hundiéndose,
tronchando obscuramente el trigal de tus canas.
Todo tú sumergido en humedad y gases
haciendo tus deshechos, tu desorden, tu alma,
cada vez más igual tu carne que tu traje,
más madera tus huesos y más huesos las tablas.
Tierra mojada donde había una boca,
aire podrido, luz aniquilada,
el silencio tendido a todo tu tamaño
germinando burbujas bajo las hojas de agua.
(Flores dominicales a dos metros arriba
te quieren pasar besos y no te pasan nada.)

Mientras los niños crecen y las horas nos hablan,
tú, subterráneamente, lentamente, te apagas.

From Something on the Death of the Eldest Sabines *(Part Two)*

I

Little by little, while the children grow,

you, with all the dead, are finishing.

Across the nights, I've been looking at you

over the marble, in your little house.

One day without eyes, nose, ears,

another day without your throat,

the skin over your forehead collapsing, sinking,

darkly breaking off in the wheat field of your gray hairs.

All of you submerged in humidity and gases,

going about your undoing, your disorder, your soul,

more and more your flesh and your suit becoming one,

your bones more wooden, and your wooden world more bony.

Where there was a mouth, wet earth,

bad air, annihilated light,

a measure of silence laid out over you

and breeding bubbles under the leaves of water.

(Six feet above, the Sunday flowers

want to pass down kisses and pass nothing.)

II

While the children grow and the hours talk to us,

underground you slowly go out.

105

Lumbre enterrada y sola, pabilo de la sombra,
veta de horror para el que te escarba.

¡Es tan fácil decirte "padre mío"
y es tan difícil encontrarte, larva
de Dios, semilla de esperanza!
Quiero llorar a veces, y no quiero
llorar porque me pasas
como un derrumbe, porque pasas
como un viento tremendo, como un escalofrío
debajo de las sábanas,
como un gusano lento a lo largo del alma.
¡Si sólo se pudiera decir: "Papá, cebolla,
polvo, cansancio, nada, nada, nada"!
¡Si con un trago se tragara!
¡Si con este dolor te apuñalara!
¡Si con este desvelo de memorias
—herida abierta, vómito de sangre—
te agarrara la cara!

Yo sé que tú ni yo,
ni un par de balbas,
ni un becerro de cobre, ni unas alas
sosteniendo la muerte, ni la espuma
en que naufraga el mar, ni—no—las playas,
la arena, la sumisa piedra con viento y agua,

Alone and buried light, wick of the darkness,
vein of horror for whoever unearths you.

It's so easy to say, "My father,"
and so hard to find you, larva
of God, seed of hope!
Sometimes I want to cry, and I don't want
to because you enter me
like a landslide, because you enter
like a tremendous wind, like a chill
under the covers,
like a slow worm along the length of my soul.
If only I could say: "Papa, onion,
dust, weariness, nothing, nothing, nothing!"
If I could swallow you with one gulp.
If I could stab you with this ache.
If in this sleeplessness of memories
—opened wound, vomit of blood—
I could hold on to your face!

I know that neither you nor I,
nor a pair of valves,
nor a copper calf, nor those wings
upholding death, nor the foam
in which the sea is wrecked, —no—nor the beaches,
the sand, the stones humbled by wind and water,

ni el árbol que es abuelo de su sombra,
ni nuestro sol, hijastro de sus ramas,
ni la fruta madura, incandescente,
ni la raíz de perlas y de escamas,
ni tu tío, ni tu chozno, ni tu hipo,
ni mi locura, y ni tus espaldas,
sabrán del tiempo oscuro que nos corre
desde las venas tibias a las canas.

(Tiempo vacío, ampolla de vinagre,
caracol recordando la resaca.)

He aquí que todo viene, todo pasa,
todo, todo se acaba.
¿Pero tú? ¿pero yo? ¿pero nosotros?
¿para qué levantamos la palabra?
¿de qué sirvió el amor?
¿cuál era la muralla
que detenía la muerte? ¿dónde estaba
el niño negro de tu guarda?

Ángeles degollados puse al pie de tu caja,
y te eché encima tierra, piedras, lágrimas,
para que ya no salgas, para que no salgas.

nor the tree that is grandfather of its shadow,

nor our sun, stepchild of the branches,

nor ripe and incandescent fruit,

nor its roots of pearls and fish scales,

nor your uncle, nor your great-grandson, nor your belch,

nor my madness, nor your shoulders,

will know of the dark time that races through us

from the lukewarm veins to the gray hairs.

(Empty time, blister of vinegar,

snail recalling the undertow.)

Here, everything comes, everything passes,

everything, everything ends.

But you? but I? but us?

why did we lift up the word?

what good was love?

which wall

held back death? where was

the black child who guarded you?

I put decapitated angels at the foot of your coffin,

and I threw earth, stones, tears on you,

so that you won't leave, so that you won't leave.

Afterword
Ernesto Trejo and the Making of *Tarumba*

This collection of the translations of the poems of Jaime Sabines has had several starts and now it has a second ending. It began back in 1968 when Mark Strand asked me to translate the poems of José Emilio Pacheco, Efraín Huerta, and Jaime Sabines for a volume he and Octavio Paz were editing to be called *New Poetry of Mexico*. Mark seemed to know I would not be excited by the work of Huerta and Pacheco, and so he offered Sabines as a lure. He was, of course, shrewd, for I fell in love with Sabines' unique voice and wild imagination, as well as his use of the vernacular. I had never before read a poet writing in Spanish who came so close to sounding like me, only a me with more daring and wit, a me obsessed with sexual love and furious that the world provided no place for it to flower. I was especially drawn to his book *Tarumba* in which he creates and addresses an alter ego who is no more and no less than his own soul wandering in the wilderness of his own lost self. I was reminded of Weldon Kees' Robinson poems, of which there are only a few; whereas Sabines had created an entire collection in which the poems were by turns morose, skeptical, outrageous, and comic, Kees' poems were consistently in the same desperate, suicidal voice. Seven of my translations—I'd done nine—appeared in the Strand/Paz collection, published in 1970. And that was that for a few years.

In the spring of 1971 the Spanish scholar and critic José Elgorriaga— then the head of the Foreign Language Department at California State University, Fresno—approached me with a proposal that together we

teach a course in translation into English of the poetry written in Spanish during the then-present century. As I was also working on the poems of Gloria Fuertes, Jorge Guillen, and Miguel de Unamuno for Hardie St. Martin's marvelous anthology *Roots and Wings*, I agreed to try it. My finest student from the previous semester, Ernesto Trejo, then pursuing a graduate degree in economics at Cal State, enrolled, and this present collection was about to get its second start. I don't really know if Ernesto discovered Sabines in that class, or if he already knew him, but when I brought to class the first draft of a new translation from the *Tarumba* poems Ernesto caught fire.

Ernesto on fire was something to behold. His brilliance and energy lit up his amazing face until I thought to myself, People this beautiful don't exist, for in truth I think Ernesto was one of the most beautiful creatures I have ever seen and by far the most beautiful person who failed to recognize his own beauty. What I did not know about Ernesto was that he was publishing poems in Spanish in his native Mexico; in truth I did not then know he was Mexican, for he had almost no accent. I should have suspected, for his English was always perfectly grammatical, a rare condition among my students educated in California's Central Valley. I made the discovery after I'd asked him where he was from; he answered Fresnillo (little Fresno, *little ash tree* in translation); I asked where that was, believing it must be a nearby town so many of which have Spanish names—Merced, Madera, Mariposa, Málaga for example. It was in the province of Zacatecas, he told me. He had come to the States at the age of seventeen. Startled, I asked why his English was so perfect; his answer was that he'd studied it in high school. (I studied French in high school and can't ask for a glass of water.)

In Los Angeles he located a copy of *Tarumba* in Spanish and began furiously translating the poems. I took up the challenge and did likewise. So each week the class would meet, and Elgorriaga would savage my translations for their inaccuracies and Ernesto's for their proximity to street English. This produced several heated arguments, for Ernesto was committed to the notion that Mexican poetry had to abandon its rhetoric and its elitism and get down to where the people spoke and lived. José was, in truth, a Spaniard as well as a dues-paying member of academia, and the cultured and hermetic voice of Juan Ramón Jiménez, the formality of Guillen, and the high-flown diction of Unamuno in no way bothered him: for him, this was modern poetry in Spanish. Both men defended their positions with passion; José felt tradition was on his side, a tradition which Ernesto found suffocating. Their biggest quarrel came when Ernesto translated a few of my poems into Spanish: "You can't do that in Spanish," José shouted. Ernesto was too civil to shout back; he merely pointed out that he had already done it, and furthermore, that Mexican poetry in the future would be in the spoken language of Mexicans.

When the semester ended, Ernesto suggested we keep working on the translations of Sabines and that instead of doing them separately we might do them together. I recognized immediately that this would make it easier for me, as I had learned Spanish in Spain from Spaniards and quite often I failed to grasp the subtleties of Mexican Spanish; nor did I even hear Mexican Spanish in my head. Castillian is far more metallic and "quick" than Mexican Spanish, which to my ear is softer and more beautiful. With the exception of the final poem in the collection, all the work in the last section of the book we did together. Before the year ended

I thought we were nearing the completion of a good-sized collection, so we applied for a grant from the Columbia Translation Center and got it. Ernesto, now married, was supporting himself as a cook in his aunt's restaurant, and the grant allowed him to devote more time to the work.

I no longer remember why it took almost six years for the completed book to be published. Ernesto went off to the University of Iowa to continue his education in the writing of poetry in English; after he got his MFA he and his family moved to Mexico City, where he was employed as an economist by the administration of López-Portillo. Twin Peaks Press of San Francisco published the original version of *Tarumba: The Selected Poems of Jaime Sabines* in 1977. The first draft of the introduction to that volume—which is also the introduction to this version—was written by Ernesto and revised by me. The owners of Twin Peaks Press (after also publishing a volume of the selected poems of the Dutch poet Rutger Kopland) moved to Holland with most of the copies of our Sabines; what became of those copies no one seems to know.

In 1983 Ernesto's family—which now included his son Victor and his daughter Kerry, as well as his wife Dianne—moved back to Fresno where Ernesto took a position teaching literature, composition, and creative writing at Fresno City College. He had already published chapbooks of his poems written in English and in Spanish, and in 1984 he published a large collection of poems in Mexico City, *El día entre las hojas* (*The Day Among the Leaves*). In 1990 Arte Público of Houston published *Entering a Life*, a collection of forty-six of his poems written in English. The voice he creates is marvelously resourceful; in the space of a few lines he can go from utter seriousness to surreal comedy; the two constants are compassion and wit. In the background one feels the

presence of Sabines, but a Sabines who has read and learned from Wallace Stevens to create a poetry like none other in English. Like Sabines he creates an alter ego, the mysterious E, though unlike Sabines he usually speaks in the voice of this imagined self:

E. CURSES THE RICH

San Teodulo, give them vinegar when they thirst.
Holy Peter, when they hunger look the other way.
St. Frigid, if they bleed have some salt on hand.
John the Baptist, drown them.
Blessed Caldron of St. Ursula, bubble in their ears...

For me his most moving poems are those in which he celebrates the boundless gifts of his ancestors, which he embodies, and those in which he turns inward to investigate that strange and mercurial creature we call the self. It is in the latter especially we encounter his astonishing gift for invention and his almost sculptural sense of exactly how the world appears:

You forgot the words and made some up. You
were confident. You knew
I would die that night yet you were confident.
You opened the door and swerved the car
at the curve. There were no such animals.
My body a still river, my head on a lagoon.
You thought you saw a swallow, a
black swallow, and still you didn't lose

115

control. The mountains to your left collapsed

and I leaped on you, where I have been ever since,

lodged somewhere between your neck and your shoulder.

(from "This Is What Happened")

Less than a year after the publication of *Entering a Life,* Ernesto was diagnosed with cancer. He fought it with all his will. "I will not roll over like a dog," he said to me. So murderous was the chemotherapy he had to take a leave from teaching. That spring it so happened that for the last time I was teaching the course in translation with José Elgorriaga. When Ernesto discovered this he asked if he could attend, which he did every week no matter how ravaged he was by the therapy. His love for poetry in Spanish and in English was so great and so obvious that on days he felt even slightly human he brought a radiance to that shabby classroom. In the spring of 1991, one week before the end of the semester and only a few days after his forty-first birthday, he died. The poetry world of Fresno has not recovered from his loss.

In 2005, having only two copies of the original version of *Tarumba* and having been asked for copies for some years, I decided to seek its republication. I have added several translations of Sabines' poems whose existence I was unaware of in 1975.

Philip Levine
Fresno, May, 2006

The Author

Jaime Sabines was born on March 25, 1926 in Chiapas, Mexico. In 1945, he relocated to Mexico City where he studied Medicine for three years before turning his attention to Philosophy and Literature at the University of Mexico. He wrote eight books of poetry, including *Horal* (1950), *Tarumba* (1956), and *Maltiempo* (1972), for which he received the Xavier Villaurrutia Award. In 1959, Sabines was granted the Chiapas Prize and, in 1983, the National Literature Award. In addition to his literary career, Sabines served as a congressman for Chiapas. Jaime Sabines died in 1999; he remains one of Mexico's most respected poets.

The Translator

Philip Levine was born in Detroit, Michigan, in 1928. He is the author of sixteen books of poetry, most recently *Breath* (Alfred A. Knopf, 2004). His other poetry collections include *The Mercy* (1999); *The Simple Truth* (1994), which won the Pulitzer Prize; *What Work Is* (1991), which won the National Book Award; *New Selected Poems* (1991); *Ashes: Poems New and Old* (1979), which received the National Book Critics Circle Award and the National Book Award for Poetry; *7 Years From Somewhere* (1979), which won the National Book Critics Circle Award; *and The Names of the Lost* (1975), which won the Lenore Marshall Poetry Prize. He has received the Ruth Lilly Poetry Prize, the Harriet Monroe Memorial Prize from *Poetry*, the Frank O'Hara Prize, and two Guggenheim Foundation fellowships. Philip Levine lives in New York City and Fresno, California, and teaches at New York University.

Jaime Sabines is a national treasure in Mexico. He is considered by
Octavio Paz to be instrumental to the genesis of modern Latin American poetry
and "one of the best poets" of the Spanish language. Toward the end of his life,
he had published for over fifty years and brought in crowds of more than 3,000
to readings in his native country. Coined the "Sniper of Literature" by Cuban
poet Roberto Fernández Retamar, Sabines brought poetry to the streets. His
vernacular, authentic poems are accessible: meant not for other poets, or the
established or elite, but for himself and for the people.

In this translation of his fourth book, *Tarumba*, we find ourselves stepping into
Sabines' streets, brothels, hospitals, and cantinas; the most bittersweet details are
told in a way that reaffirms that "life bursts from you, like scarlet fever, without
warning." Eloquently co-translated by Philip Levine and the late Ernesto Trejo,
this bilingual edition is a classic for Spanish- and English-speaking readers alike.
Secretive, wild, and searching, these poems are rife with such intensity you'll feel
"heaven is sucking you up through the roof."

Books

www.sarabandebooks.org

ISBN 13: 978-1-932511-48-2

51495

9 781932 511482

Poetry / $14.95